Anonymous

The Unlawfulness Polygamy Evinced

Or, observations occasioned by the erroneous interpretations of the

passages of the New Testament, respecting the laws of marriage lately

published in a treatise on female ruin

Anonymous

The Unlawfulness Polygamy Evinced
*Or, observations occasioned by the erroneous interpretations of the passages of the
New Testament, respecting the laws of marriage lately published in a treatise on
female ruin*

ISBN/EAN: 9783337307950

Printed in Europe, USA, Canada, Australia, Japan

Cover: Foto ©Lupo / pixelio.de

More available books at **www.hansebooks.com**

THE

UNLAWFULNESS

OF

POLYGAMY

EVINCED.

[Price, One Shilling and Sixpence.]

THE

UNLAWFULNESS

OF

POLYGAMY

EVINCED:

OR,

OBSERVATIONS

OCCASIONED BY THE

ERRONEOUS INTERPRETATIONS

OF THE PASSAGES OF THE

NEW TESTAMENT,

RESPECTING THE

LAWS OF MARRIAGE,

Lately publifhed in a Treatife on

FEMALE RUIN.

———————————

LONDON:

Printed for G. KEARSLY, Fleet-ftreet,

M.DCC.LXXX.

THE READER.

THE following Obfervations are offered
from Motives of fincere Regard for the
prefent and future Happinefs of Mankind.
They are defigned to remind you of
the true Meaning of the Paffages of the
New Teftament refpecting the Laws of
Marriage, and to obviate the erroneous
Interpretations of them lately publifhed in
the Treatife on Female Ruin. A Treatife
which the Author of thefe Obfervations
hath been induced to confider, not from
any Apprehenfions of the Influence of it
upon the fincere Chriftian acquainted with
the Senfe of the facred Writings, but from
a View of the Illufion, and Encouragement
that may refult from it to the Uninformed,
the Prejudiced, and Vicious.

Perfons

Perfons of this Defcription will ever be difpofed to credit Suggeftions that favour their Condu&t, and would gladly intrench themfelves under the San&tion and Authority of a Preacher of the Gofpel, in the prefent Cafe, however averfe they may be from attending to his Inftru&ions in other Inftances.

That the following Obfervations may eonduce to the Promotion of the Purpofes for which they are offered, is the Obje&t of the fincereft Wifhes of your, *&c.*

H. W.

London,
Oct. 3, 1780.

THE

UNLAWFULNESS

OF

POLYGAMY

EVINCED.

THE Author of Thelyphthora having afferted that Polygamy ' allowed by the Law of Mofes, is not prohibited by the Gofpel,' and that it was impoffible that our bleffed Lord, who came not to deftroy the Law, but to fulfil it, fhould condemn Polygamy as Adultery, we fhall only confider and obviate this Writer's erroneous Interpretations of the Paffages of the New Teftament refpecting thofe Points.

For if thefe Paffages of the New Teftament are found to afford no Foundation for our Author's Pofitions, he muft appear to have been

but

but erecting a Caftle in the Air, and, after all the Expence of Labour he hath incurred, his mighty and elaborate Superftructure muft fall to the Ground. Moft certainly, nothing lefs than the Authority of Revelation can determine on the Points here treated; the facred Writings are our only certain Rule of Faith and Conduct, and to no Truths fhould we more readily fubfcribe than to thefe afferted by thofe early Writers of the Church, who, notwithftanding their Errors are acknowledged, by one, who was as little partial to them as our Author, to have been 'the chief Ornaments of the Ages in which they lived;' " that we are not to attend to human Affertions, but to eftablifh our Queftions by the Scriptures, which are our moft certain, μαλλον η μονη αποδειξις, or rather our only Demonftration of the Truth of them; and that Δει παν ρημα η πραγμα πιςουσθαι τη μηρτυρια της Θεοπνευςυ γραφης : every Affertion and Action, or every Thing that is faid or done, ought to be confirmed by the Evidence of the divinely-infpired Writings."—*Clemens Alex. Strom. Bafil Ethu.*

Let us proceed to the Confideration of the Paffages of the New Teftament erroneoufly interpreted

terpreted by our Author. The Author of Thelyphthora afferts that our bleffed Lord's Difcourfes, in the Beginning of the nineteenth Chapter of St. Matthew, and of the tenth of St. Mark, as well as in other Parts of the New Teftament, concerning the Laws of Marriage, relate only to Divorce, yet muft we affirm that they alfo condemn Polygamy; and that Polygamy allowed by the Law, is therefore forbidden under the Gofpel. The Truth of thefe Pofitions, muft evidently appear to all who impartially review thofe Paffages.

' The Pharifees came to our Lord tempting him, and faying unto him; Is it lawful for a Man to put away his Wife for every Caufe? And he anfwered, and faid unto them, Have ye not read, that he who made them at the Beginning, made them Male, and Female?' As though he had faid, have ye not read, in the Mofaic Account of the Creation, that God, from the Beginning of it, when he certainly conftituted human Nature in a Way moft conducive to your Happinefs, in creating your firft Parents, made them Male and Female, or one Man, and one Woman, which would neither allow of Divorce or Polygamy? ' And faid, for

B   this

this Caufe fhall a Man leave Father and Mother, and fhall adhere to his Wife, and they two fhall be one Flefh; wherefore they are no longer two, but one Flefh; what therefore God hath joined together, faith he, under the Difpenfation of the Gofpel, let not Man feparate, or put afunder.' Let the Bond of Matrimony be efteemed fuch as nothing can diffolve, except what can make them ceafe to be one Flefh by rendering the Perfon of one, common to fome third Perfon. They are not to be feparated unlefs they have rendered themfelves one Flefh with fome other.

' They fay unto him, Why then did Mofes command to give a Writing of Divorcement, and to difmifs or put her away? He faith unto them, Mofes, becaufe of the Hardnefs of your Hearts, fuffered you to put away your Wives; but from the Beginning it was not fo; and I, who appear to reduce this Inftitution to its original Perfection, fay unto you, that, under the Difpenfation of the Gofpel, ' Whofoever fhall put away his Wife, except it be for Fornication, and fhall marry another, committeth Adultery; and whofo marrieth her that is put away, committeth Adultery.' The fame Truths our Lord
alfo

also afferts in the fifth of St. Matthew and fix-
teenth of St. Luke: in the former, explaining
the Law, he faith, that 'whofoever fhall put
away his Wife, faving for the Caufe of Fornication, caufeth her to commit Adultery;' and
whofoever fhall marry her that is divorced,
committeth Adultery; in the latter, our Lord,
afferting the Law in its utmoft Extent, and
Spirituality, affirms, that fuch unjuft Difmiffion
of a Wife, and marrying another, were contrary
to the original Defign of Marriage and Adultery; for, 'whofoever, putteth away his Wife
and marrieth another, faith he, committeth
Adultery: and whofoever marrieth her that is
put away from her Hufband, committeth Adultery.'

Upon our Lord having made fuch exprefs
Declaration, St. Matthew relates that his Difciples fay unto him, if the Cafe of a Man be fo
with his Wife, it is not good to marry. But
he faid unto them, all Men cannot receive this
Saying, fave they to whom it is given.

With this Relation of St. Matthew, refpeƈt-
ing the Points before us, let us review that of
St. Mark. The Pharifees, faith this Evan-

gelift,

gelift, came to our Lord, and afked him, Is it lawful for a man to put away his Wife? tempting him, conceiving that his Reply might adminifter fome Pretence for Cenfure. And he anfwered and faid unto them, What did Mofes command you? And they faid, Mofes fuffered to write a Bill of Divorcement, and to put her away: And Jefus anfwered, and faid unto them, for the Hardnefs of your Heart, which prevented your perceiving and adhering to the firft Inftitution and original Defign of Matrimony, he wrote you this Precept. But from the Beginning of the Creation, God would have it otherwife, for he made them Male and Female. For this Caufe fhall a Man leave his Father and Mother, and adhere to his Wife; and they twain fhall be one Flefh; fo then they are no more twain, or two, but one Flefh: What, therefore, God hath thus joined together, let no Man, under the Difpenfation of the Gofpel, pretend to put afunder. And, when in the Houfe, his Difciples afked him again of the fame Matter: And he faith to them, that according to the original Defign of Marriage, ' Whofoever fhall put away his Wife, and marry another, committeth Adultery againft her,' fhe, by the primitive Inftitution

of

of the conjugal Union being ftill his Wife, and having the fole Right to his Perfon; ' And if a Woman fhall put away her Hufband, and be married to another, fhe committeth Adultery.'

From the preceding Paffages nothing can be more evident to an impartial Reader, than that our bleffed Lord was fpeaking of the primitive Inftitution of Marriage; that he would have his Difciples act according to the original Defign of it; that he hath reduced the Law of Marriage to that primitive Inftitution which would not admit of Divorce or Polygamy; that Man and Wife are by perfonal Union one Flefh, and cannot be feparated except for perfonal Intercourfe with fome other; that whofoever fhall put away his Wife and marry another, except for Fornication, committeth Adultery againft her; and if a Woman fhall put away her Hufband, and be married to another, fhe committeth Adultery, the Hufband and Wife having by the original Inftitution of Marriage the fole Right to each other's Perfon: that not only the Hufband hath the fole Right to the Perfon of his Wife, but that fhe alfo hath the fole Right to the Perfon of her Hufband: according to St. Paul's exprefs Commands, where he faith to

avoid

avoid Fornication, let every Man have his own Wife, and every Woman her own Hufband.— " Let the Hufband render unto the Wife due Benevolence, and likewife the Wife unto the Hufband. The Wife hath not Power over her own Body, but the Hufband; and likewife the Hufband hath not Power over his own Body, but the Wife :" their Engagements being reciprocal, they are in Confcience obliged to continue appropriate to each other.

With refpect to the Remark of the Author of Thelyphthora, upon the Difference of Expreffion in the original Words, εαυτε γυναικα and τον ιδιου ανδρα, which might be rendered, Let every Man have his own Wife, and every Woman her own proper Hufband.—The Difference may as well denote fuch an Appropriation of the Hufband to the Wife, that he have no perfonal Intercourfe with any other Woman, as that fhe fhould not have perfonal Intercourfe with any other Man ; and nothing can be more evident than the Unlawfulnefs of Polygamy from thefe Paffages of St. Paul. For, if the Hufband hath not Power over his own Body, but the Wife, he, certainly, cannot transfer that Power by marrying another. We may alfo here add, that however the Au-
                                                            thor

thor of Thelyphthora may conceive that Doctor Whitby's Prejudices have warred against his Judgment, in his Note upon the 10th Chapter of St. Mark's Gofpel, and that he hath there found out "a *plain* Argument against Things not mentioned or even hinted at in the Text," we muft beg Leave to obferve, that that learned Commentator by no Means appears to have erred refpecting the Intention and Meaning of our Lord in that Chapter, and that really Judgment, and not Prejudice, dictated the Comment.

That learned Writer, in the Words immediately preceding, and which are a Part of the Note that the Author of Thelyphthora hath quoted, faith, that from our Lord's Declaration, that he who putteth away his Wife and marrieth another, committeth Adultery against her, it clearly follows, 'that he who not having put her away marries another, muft be guilty of the fame Crime, feeing he muft have the fame Power to marry another when the firft is put away, as when fhe is not put away.' And then follows the reft of the Note. What can more clearly refer to not only the Unlawfulnefs of Divorce, but alfo of Polygamy, and more evi-

4   dently

dently condemn Polygamy as Adultery, than
such an exprefs Declaration, that whofoever
difmiffeth his Wife and marrieth another, committeth Adultery againft her ?—And what can
be more evident from the preceding Relations
of the Evangelifts, and Declarations of the
Apoftle, than the Obligations of Hufband and
Wife to continue entirely appropriate to each
other, and that our bleffed Lord in his Reply to
the Pharifees, referred to the original Defign of
the conjugal Union, and hath reduced the
Laws of it to the primitive Inftitution of Matrimony ?

With refpect to the Beginning of the firft
Chapter of Deuteronomy, be it tranflated im-
peratively, or as our Author defires, hypothe-
tically, yet, have we our Saviour's Authority to
affert that, " for the Hardnefs of their Hearts
Mofes wrote them the Precept concerning Divorce, and fuffered them to difmifs their Wives,
but from the *Beginning* it was not fo."

Mofes, not as a Politician, as our Author
would fuggeft, but as a Lawgiver, as God's
Minifter permitted Divorce.   This was a divine
Permiffion,

Permiffion, and therefore the Deity difpenfed
with his own Inftitution.

The Jews were permitted to difmifs their
Wives, for fome Matter of Uncleannefs. This
Caufe of Divorce was certainly fomething lefs
than Fornication, becaufe our Lord condemns
it as an unjuft Caufe of Difmiffion, and yet permits Divorce in cafe of Fornication. Perhaps
this Caufe was neither what the Schools of Hil-
lel nor Shammai adopted; and as our Lord allows Divorce in cafe of Adultery, and Adultery was punifhed with Death, the Caufe of
Divorce permitted under the Old Teftament,
muft have been fomething between their Interpretations. Be it however what it may, it was
permitted, and Chrift only faith that under the
Difpenfation of the Gofpel it fhould not obtain,
but that Chriftians muft act according to *his*
Law refpecting it, who hath reduced Matrimony
to its primitive Inftitution.

With relation to the Old Teftament, our
Lord here hath certainly prefcribed a *new* Law,
which had not before obtained among the Jews.
Divorces under the Old Teftament were permitted for lefs Caufes than Fornication; but

our

our Saviour under the Gofpel will not permit
them, except in that Cafe. The Anfwer of
Chrift to the Pharifees refpecting Divorce was,
as our Author allows, ‘ grounded on the old
Marriage Inftitution;’ and this, with relation
to the Law, is certainly a *new* Difpenfation.

Our Author, endeavouring to evade the
Force of the twenty-eighth Verfe of the fifth
Chapter of St. Matthew’s Gofpel, affirms, that
the Word Woman in the Original muft mean
fuch a Woman as Adultery could be committed
with, fuppofing the Thought brought forth
into Act, p. 124. Let us review this Paffage.
‘ Whofoever looketh upon a Woman to luft after
her, hath already committed Adultery with her
in his Heart.’ The evident Meaning of thefe
Words is, that whofoever fhall gaze on a Woman to luft after her, and inftead of rejecting,
indulge the fecret Workings of Defire, or purpofe alfo to gratify it, hath already committed
Adultery with her in his Heart, he only having
efcaped for want of Opportunity to accomplifh
his irregular Defire. It is well known that the
Word here tranflated ‘ looketh on,’ means to
gaze on, or fix the Eye with the utmoft Attention upon : nor can any Thing be more evident
than

than that the original Word that is here tranflated 'a Woman,' is, like נשה, a general
Term, that diftinguifheth a Woman from a
Man. Yet the Author of Thelyphthora would
have us think, that the Word Woman here muft
certainly mean a Woman who is either efpoufed
or hath cohabited with her Hufband, (p. 124);
as if Adultery could be committed with no
other: and the Reafon he gives for fuch Interpretation, and his Inference from it, feem wor-
thy the Attention of all Polygamifts, that they
may perceive not only by what found Criticifm,
but alfo by what powerful Evidence of Reafon
and Revelation their Caufe can be fupported.

Our Author, aware that if he cannot limit
the Word Woman in this Paffage to an efpoufed
or married Woman, the marrying two or three,
or indeed more than one Virgin or Widow at
once, muft be here condemned as Adultery,
hath very confiftently with his Attempts upon
other Paffages, hereafter to be confidered, endeavoured to perfuade us, that the original
Word here tranflated Woman, " cannot mean
a Woman as generally diftinguifhed from a
Man; for, faith he, if it be finful to look with
Defire on any Woman *whatfoever*, then it would

be finful for a Man to defire his own Wife to
whom he is lawfully married, or a Virgin to
whom he is contracted; and this, faith our Author, (who is particularly fond of running out
into Confequences, and entertaining and well-
known Anecdotes and Fables), would lead us
into all the Abfurdities of the ancient Mifoga-
mifts, who held Marriage to be finful. In this
Place, therefore, proceeds he, it certainly
means a Woman confidered as related to a Man,
and that whether efpoufed, or that hath cohabited with her Hufband, for with no other *can*
Adultery be committed. For want of fuch
Diftinction, fome Commentators, adds he, by
letting loofe their own Imaginations, have filled
many of their Readers with Matter of fore
Diftrefs and Bondage of Confcience, as if the
Defire after any Female whatfoever came within
what they call the fpiritual Import of the Se-
venth Commandment." P. 121. But our Author, in endeavouring to releafe us from thefe
Matters of *fore* Diftrefs and *Bondage* of Confcience, with which, for want of his *recondite*
Diftinction, fome, I would fay the Bulk of the
moft judicious and learned Commentators, ' have
filled us,' unhappily hath really let loofe his
own Imagination, and made a Diftinction where

no Difference fubfifts, and hath proceeded fo far
as to advance a Pofition that hath no Foundation in the New Teftament, even at the Expence of impeaching the Truth of his own preceding Affertions.

Our Author here exprefsly contradicts himfelf. For, in p. 42, he afferts, " that there are
no fpecific Names for married Perfons in the
Old or New Teftament, but only Words for a
Man and Woman, that fignify Perfons of the
male and female Sex in general; but when
coupled with Pronouns poffeffive, as ο ανηρ σου,
thy Man, and η γυνη αυτε, his Woman, they
denote the marriage Relation."

Such being our Author's Conceffion, let us
review the Original of this Paffage of St.
Matthew, and fee whether any Pronoun poffeffive is coupled in it with the original Word
for a Woman, or it means according to his
Rule, only a Woman, or Female in general.

The original Words need only be read to
fettle this Point, and are thefe, Εγω δε λεγω υμιν
οτι πας ο βλεπων γυναικα προς το επιθυμησαι αυτης,
ηδη εμοιχευσεν αυτην εν τη καρδια αυτε——

4   The

The Words here being οβλεπων γυναικα without any Pronoun poſſeſſive coupled with γυναικα, or a Woman, according to our Author's own Rule, muſt mean any Woman in general, be ſhe Virgin, Widow or Wife. Such are the extraordinary Obſervations and Deductions of our Author reſpecting this Paſſage of Scripture; in farther Reply to which, we muſt therefore remind him, that it moſt evidently condemns the perſonal Intercourſe of a married Man with any unmarried Woman; that it moſt certainly proves that the Deſire after any Female in general, except his own Wife, comes within what is called the ſpiritual Import of the ſeventh Commandment, that it condemns all Polygamy as Adultery, and therefore evinceth the Error of our Author's Aſſertion, that Adultery cannot be committed with any but an eſpouſed or married Woman. Adultery certainly cannot be committed in the Inſtance mentioned by the Author of Thelyphthora; though it hath been ſuggeſted, that a Caſe might occur in which a Man could be guilty of a Breach of the ſeventh Commandment, with his own Wife. But we ſhall decline the Conſideration of ſuch Inſtance, and all viſionary Refinements reſpecting it, nor particularly take Notice of this Writer's ex-

traordinary

traordinary Suggeftion, that " the Word Woman, here, muft fignify a married Woman, or
elfe a Man who looks with Defire on his Wife,
muft commit Adultery with her;" as if any
Woman in *general*, meant any Woman *whatfoever*, and no general Term allowed of any Ex-
ception. Difmiffing fuch merely illufive Quib-
bles, and evafive Artifices, let us readily grant
that the Woman here meant, muft be fuch an
one as Adultery can be committed with; and
remind our Reader, that the Author, when he
defined Adultery to be the Commerce of
the Sexes where the Woman is the Wife of another Man, p. 57, fhould have truly completed
the Definition; by adding alfo that it is the
Commerce of the Sexes where the Man is the
Hufband of another Woman: for our bleffed
Lord hath exprefsly declared, that whofoever
putteth away his Wife and marrieth another, or
hath Commerce with another, committeth
Adultery againft her, his firft Wife.

No matter, therefore, whether the Woman
defired be married or not; for if the Man who
looks with Defire on her, be married, he committeth Adultery in his Heart; and if an unmarried Man thus looks with Defire on a
Woman

Woman with whom Adultery can be committed, that is, on a married Woman, *he*, alfo, committeth Adultery with her in his Heart. Not both, but one of the Parties undoubtedly, muft, be married, ·as we cannot fuppofe our Saviour to be here prefcribing a Law againft a Cafe, or Inftance that can never fubfift. But yet, nothing can be more evident from our Lord's Words than, that whofoever looketh with Defire on a Woman with whom he can commit Adultery, a married Woman, or a fingle Woman, if he be married, the Word Woman denoting all Women in general, is an Adulterer, or hath already committed Adultery with her in his Heart.

Our Author's Diftinction, therefore, hath here no Foundation; nor have our Commentators let loofe their Imaginations beyond the Truth, though they have declared that the irregular Defire after any Female whatfoever, with whom Adultery can be committed, comes within the fpiritual Import of the feventh Commandment. Nor can any thing hence be more evident, than that Polygamy is a fin under the Difpenfation of the Gofpel, and that therefore the Prohibition of it *hath Warrant*
from

from the Word of God. For as our Saviour hath here exprefsly affured us, that whofoever looketh with irregular Defire after any Woman with whom Adultery can be committed, hath already committed Adultery with her in his Heart; moft certainly he who marrieth, or hath perfonal Intercourfe with her, muft alfo be guilty of Adultery. With refpect to the Conduct of the Patriarchs, and other Saints who lived before the Promulgation of the Gofpel, we fhall not enquire into it, nor confider for what Reafons Polygamy was then permitted. Their Example is by no Means in every refpect the Object of our Attention.

The Pattern of our bleffed Lord is the only Object intitled to our Imitation, as it exemplifies fuch a complete and perfect Plan of Piety and Morality, as was never before his Incarnation vouchfafed to Mankind. Our Author may be averfe from fubfcribing to this Truth, but hath afforded us an acceffional Proof of it. For as the Gofpel enjoins a purer Conduct, and prohibits all Polygamy which was permitted by the Old Teftament, fuch Prohibition evinceth the Superiority of the Rule prefcribed to our Behaviour in the former, to that of the latter.

D   It

It appears alſo, from the Paſſages adduced, that, contrary to our Author's Aſſertions, the Thought of Adultery and Polygamy were really *firſt condemned* when Chriſt ſaid, whoſoever look-'eth on a Woman to luſt after her, hath already committed Adultery with her in his Heart; and that Adultery, therefore, meant not " *quite as much in Moſes's Time, as in the Days of Chriſt and his Apoſtles;*" that the Thought of Adultery, when Polygamy was permitted, was *not* ſo ſinful as it would have been in St. Paul under the Goſpel; that the Scribes and Phariſees were ig-norant of the ſpiritual Senſe of the Law; that our Saviour informed them, that unjuſt Divorce and Polygamy were unlawful under his Diſpen-ſation; that not only our exterior Conduct, but our very Thoughts, might be ſinful and adul-terous, which the Law that forbad them to co-vet was not underſtood by them to mean; and that therefore our Lord hath introduced a new Law or Direction concerning thoſe Points.

The Author of Thelyphthora, in Page 192, aſſerts, that ' it is propable that Polygamy was very frequent amongſt the firſt Chriſtians.' ' Why, ſaith he, did Paul recommend the Choice of Biſhops from amongſt thoſe who had

but

but one Wife? What Occasion for this Caution, if none had more than one?'—In Reply to this Assertion, it might be observed, that after all Suggestions respecting the admitting Converts to the Rites of the Church, who were Polygamists, it might, perhaps, be supported, that not every Man who had long been in Habits of Vice, and Error, could, at once, relinquish them, and perfectly conform, in every Instance, to so pure and strict a Rule of Behaviour as that of the Gospel; and that the divine Wisdom might at first, therefore, avoid too great Rigour in condemning Polygamy, and yet fix such a Mark of Infamy upon so irregular a Practice, as to forbid any one, however extraordinary his Character might be, to undertake the Ministry, who was guilty of it; and also to discourage and condemn it by express Injunctions against it.

This, it is to be confessed, may appear a larger Concession than is necessary in the present Case. For the Injunction of one Wife refers by no Means to the Conduct of the first Christians after their Conversion, but to the Practices of the Jews and Pagans; and we have no Authority from Scripture to assert, that the first Chris-

tians

..ans were permitted to be Polygamifts, but as our Lord and his Apoftles have fo particularly prohibited it, have Reafon to believe that they conformed to their Prohibitions refpecting it.

The Words of the Apoftle by no Means authorife us to affert, that the firft, or many of the firft Chriftians, were Polygamifts after their Converfion. We are very fenfible that at the Time when St. Paul wrote the Epiftle to Timothy before us, many of the Jews and Pagans were Polygamifts, and alfo particularly guilty of unjuftly divorcing their Wives, and marrying others. And, from our Knowledge of this Practice, we learn the true Senfe of the Paffage before us, in which he enjoins that a Bifhop be the Hufband of one Wife; which is this, that he have avoideth the Practice of the Jews and Greeks, and not, like them, been guilty of unjuftly divorcing one Wife, and marrying another. The Paffage therefore evidently refers, not to the Practices of the firft Chriftians after their Converfion, but to thofe of the Jews and Pagans; and, inftead of advancing, directly militates againft Polygamy, or the Suppofition that the firft Chriftians were guilty of it, by enjoining that a Bifhop be not one who hath un-

juftly

juſtly divorced one Wife, and married another, or that in this reſpect he be the Huſband of one Wife, which he could not be if he had married a ſecond Wife during the Life of the firſt, whom he had unjuſtly diſmiſſed.

The Apoſtle's Words in this Paſſage, therefore, *carry no tacit Allowance* of Polygamy, but a direct Prohibition of it, and an obvious Reference to the Practices of the Jews and Greeks, who were guilty of Polygamy and unlawful Divorces, which he forbids as inconſiſtent with the Conduct of a Chriſtian Paſtor, and the Purity of Manners enjoined by the Goſpel; and our Author, indeed, might as well have inferred from the Injunctions of St. Paul in this Chapter, that a Biſhop ought to be no Striker, not given to much Wine, and not covetous; that Wrath, Intemperance and Covetouſneſs, were frequent amongſt the firſt Chriſtians, as that they were Polygamiſts, and conſtrue every Prohibition of Vice into a tacit Allowance of it, and an Impeachment of the Conduct of all to whom it was addreſſed.

But let us attend to our Writer's Remarks upon Part of the Seventh Chapter of the Firſt

Epiſtle

Epiftle to the Corinthians. The Apoftle in this Chapter anfwered fome Queftions of the Corinthians refpecting the conjugal State, and in the introductory Verfes determines that in fome Cafes it fhould be entered into, and continued in, and in others avoided. ' Neverthelefs, to avoid, or on Account of Fornications, faith the Apoftle, let every Man have, or retain his own Wife; and let every Woman have, and retain her own proper Hufband. Let the Hufband render due Benevolence to the Wife, and in like Manner alfo the Wife unto the Hufband. For the Wife hath not Power over her own Body, but the Hufband; and the Hufband hath not Power over his own Body, but the Wife—their Engagements being mutual, they are obliged to remain appropriate to each other.' Our Author paraphrafes thefe Words thus : ' Let every Man retain the Woman who belongs to him, and not lend her out or fuffer her to marry another, nor let him take a Woman who is not his Wife, but another Man's, to himfelf. So alfo let every Woman have her own proper Hufband; the Man appropriated to her exclufively of all other Men upon Earth, and not depart, or fuffer herfelf to be lent or given to any other Man. Let the Hufband render to the Wife due

Benevo-

Benevolence, and likewife the Wife unto the Hufband. The Wife hath not Power over her own Body, fo as to withdraw herfelf from the conjugal Debt; but the Hufband may, as Matter of Right, have Accefs to her at all proper Times and Seafons. Likewife the Hufband has not Power over his own Body, fo as to withdraw from the conjugal Intercourfe, with his Wife; but the Wife, as a Debt due from the Contract which the Man is under to her by the very Terms of their Union, has a Right to his Society. Therefore defraud ye not one the other, &c.'

With refpect to this our Author's Paraphrafe, it may be obferved, that the Word in the Original, here tranflated *have* or retain, (in the Verfe, " Let every Man *have* his own Wife, and every Woman *have* her own proper Hufband,") is the fame in both Parts of the Verfe; and therefore fhould convey the fame Ideas or Injunction, when it coheres with the Words ' every Woman,' or the Wife, as when it agrees with the Words ' every Man,' or the Hufband. Our Author, therefore, had no Authority from the Original to fuggeft that the Apoftle in thefe Paffages intended to impofe any greater Reftraint upon the Wife than upon the Hufband; but

but that, as he here enjoins that every Man fhall
have his own Wife, and not lend her out, or
fuffer her to marry another Man; fo, alfo, he
enjoins that every Woman fhall have her own
proper Hufband, and not fuffer *him* to be lent
out, or marry any other Woman.

We may hence alfo obferve, that the original
Words, here tranflated ' her own proper Hufband,' imply, as before remarked, not only
fuch an Appropriation of the Hufband to the
Wife, as that *fhe* fhould not go to any other,
but more naturally and obvioufly, fuch an Appropriation of the Hufband to the Wife, exclufively of all other Women, that *he* fhould not
marry, or have perfonal Intercourfe with any
other; and that our Author had no Ground for
the Limitation here introduced, by fubjoining
the Apoftle's Injunction, a Prohibition extending to *only* a matrimonial Connexion with ' another Man's Wife :' when a married Man,
during the Life of his firft Wife, except in cafe
of lawful Divorce, hath no Power to marry, or
have perfonal Intercourfe with any other, but is
obliged to remain appropriated to his firft Wife,
exclufively of all other Women whatfoever.

We

We readily grant, that the Corinthians were guilty of Fornication and Adultery, of lending out their Wives, and having Women in common. Let us add, that they also, as well as other Heathens, and the Jews, were guilty of Divorce and Polygamy.

Yet, what one Deduction can hence be derived in favour of Polygamy? And, what can more evidently evince the Unlawfulnefs of Polygamy than the Paffages of St. Paul before us?

If, according to our Author's Rule, we interpret them by the general Tenor of the New Teftament, nothing can more plainly evince the Unlawfulnefs of Polygamy.

The general Tenor of the Declarations of our bleffed Lord and his Apoftles, is, that whofoever difmiffeth his Wife, except for Fornication, and marrieth another, committeth Adultery againft her, and that we are to conform to the primitive Inftitution of Matrimony, which could not permit Polygamy. The Apoftle, therefore, by commanding that every Man fhould have or retain his own Wife, and

E   every

every Woman her own proper Hufband, muft
certainly mean to forbid not only all Fornication, and unjuft Divorce, but alfo all Adultery and Polygamy. The fame Truth is glare-
ingly evident alfo, from the fubfequent Words
that ‘ the Wife hath not Power over her own
Body, but the Hufband:’ and, in *like Manner*,
alfo, ‘ the Hufband hath not Power over *his*
own Body, but the Wife ;’ they being obliged
to continue appropriate to each other. It hence
evidently appears that the Wife’s Right is equal
to that of the Hufband, expreffed in exactly
the fame Words and declared to be the fame,
ομοιως δε και ο ανηρ, and that as the Hufband
hath Power over the Perfon of the Wife, fo
alfo, in like Manner, hath the Wife Power
over the Perfon of her Hufband. That therefore alfo the original Words ιδιον ανδρα and εαυτω
γυναικα, rendered her own proper Hufband, and
his own Wife, after all, mean but the fame
Thing, unlefs the Difference was made with a
particular View to the Difcouragement of Polygamy, and unjuft Divorce, and evince her
peculiar Right to the *whole* Perfon of her
Hufband.

Certainly,

Certainly, fuch are the Laws of Chrift, and his Apoftles, concerning " the Bufinefs of Divorce and Polygamy," which therefore, contrary to our Author's Affertion, depend *not* " *wholly* upon the Law of Mofes." Mofes permitted Polygamy, and unjuft Divorce; Chrift prohibits both, and hath reduced Marriage to its primitive Inftitution ; therefore he hath certainly introduced a new, or another Law refpecting them.

With regard to our Author's Affertion, that St. Paul's Injunction concerning the Choice of the Paftors of the Church, muft imply that there were many Chriftians, ' *not who had had*, but who, at the Time *when he wrote*, had more Wives than one;' and that ' if this had not been the Cafe, it would have been as much out of the Queftion to have mentioned the having but one Wife, as to have faid that none fhould be chofen but thofe who had but one Head, or one Body, when it was not to be fuppofed that any Man had more.' P. 205.

Be it obferved, that the Cafe is not parallel, for though we cannot fuppofe a Man to have more than one Head, or Body, yet he certainly might have not been fit for the Miniftry, as he

might

might have been one who had divorced one Wife, and married another; and therefore not fo blamelefs and irreproachable, as the Apoftle requires him to be. As to our Author's Remark, that the Injunction of the Apoftle muft imply that many of the firft Converts to Chriftianity were Polygamifts, becaufe in his Epiftle to Titus the Words are, Εἰ τις ἐϛιν μιας γυναικος ανδρα; ' if any *be* the Hufband of one Wife,' and therefore muft relate to the *then* Situation of the Converts to Chriftianity; it is to be obferved, that our Author hath here omitted a Word in this Paffage. For St. Paul, directing Titus on what Principles he fhould proceed in the Choice of Chriftian Paftors, here faith, Εἰ τις ἐϛιν ανεβκλητος, μιας γυναικος ανερ—' If any one be blamelefs; the Hufband of one Wife.' This Omiffion, it is prefumed, was intended to more clofely connect the εἰ τις ἐϛιν with μιας γυναικος ανδρα, and thus caufe the Apoftle to appear to more ftrongly fpeak to our Writer's Purpofe.

But this is not the Apoftle's Intention; for though the Word ἐϛιν, or *be*, is here ufed in the prefent Tenfe, yet the Paffage, as before evinced, refers not to the Polygamy of Chriftians after their Converfion, but to the then Situation of Jews and Pagans, and the former Conduct

duct of thofe Converts who had been guilty of
Polygamy or unlawful Divorce before their
Converfion, and therefore *had had* more than
one Wife; and accordingly the Apoftle, who
required that the Paftors of the Chriftian Church
fhould be Perfons of exemplary Purity, and
eminent for every focial and perfonal Virtue,
enjoins that they be not chofen from amongft
thofe who had had more than one Wife, or unjuftly difmiffed one and married another; but
that if a Perfon *be* the Hufband of one Wife,
i. e. hath not *unjuftly* difmiffed one Wife and
married another, he might be conftituted a
Bifhop.

Our Author's Pofition therefore hath no
Foundation from the Paffage before us; and I
conceive that we might as well fuppofe that all
the firft Chriftians were guilty after their Converfion, of Extortion, Theft, Covetoufnefs, Ido-
latry, and of all other Vices mentioned in St.
Paul's firft Epiftle to the Corinthians, as of
Polygamy. But St. Paul hath affured us to
the contrary; and having particularly mentioned
Fornicators, Whoremongers, and Adulterers,
as well as Perfons who were guilty of the preceding Vices, informs us, that fuch were fome
of

of the Corinthians in their unconverted State, but that divine Crace had produced an happy Change in their State and Difpofition, and they were now, fince their Converfion, wafhed, fanctified, and purified.

Our Author obferves upon thefe Paffages of St. Paul, that it can hardly be fuppofed that if Polygamy were finful, the great Apoftle fhould be fo liberal and particular in his Epiftle to the Corinthians, in contemning other Species of illicit Commerce between the Sexes, and yet omit this in his black Catalogue. In Reply to this Suggeftion, we muft obferve, that though the Apoftle hath not inferted the Word Polygamy in that Catalogue, yet hath he, by no Means, omitted to condemn the Crime it denotes.

For the Apoftle in the Paffages before us precautions the Corinthians of the fatal Effects of thofe Sins in which they had indulged themfelves before their Converfion, and againft all vain Imaginations that their having embraced Chriftianity would fecure them in the Practice of them. ' Be not deceived, faith he, neither Fornicators, nor Idolators, nor Adulterers, nor

4   Effeminate,

Effeminate, nor Abusers of themselves with Mankind, nor Thieves, nor Covetous, nor Drunkards, nor Revilers, nor Extortioners, shall inherit the Kingdom of God, and such were some of you, but ye are washed, but ye are sanctified, but ye are justified in the Name of our Lord Jesus, and by the Spirit of our God.' Polygamy, a Community of Women, Divorce and Adultery, being, confessedly, the Crimes of which the Corinthians were guilty before their Conversion, and that occasioned this Epistle of St. Paul, most certainly, he hath here shewn his Zeal for the Law of Marriage, and condemned Polygamy as well as other Species of illicit Commerce between the Sexes, when he assureth them, that neither Fornicators nor Adulterers shall inherit the Kingdom of God. If our Judgment respecting the Meaning of the Apostle should, as our Author agrees, be directed by the Consideration of the Manners and Customs of the Corinthians, and the Tenour of the New Testament; the lending their Wives, a Community of Women, Divorce and Polygamy, being, at the Time St. Paul wrote, the Crimes they were guilty of; and this Apostle having declared that the Husband hath no Power to transfer his Person to a second Wife

F   during

during the Life of his firſt, and our bleſſed
Lord having, in various Paſſages, expreſsly
aſſerted, that whoſoever ſhall unjuſtly diſmiſs
his Wife, and marry another, committeth Adultery againſt her, St. Paul muſt have conſidered
Polygamy as Adultery, and therefore, when he
here condemns Fornication and Adultery, he
condemns Polygamy as well as other Species of
illicit Commerce of the Sexes. If farther Proofs
need be adduced, evincing that St. Paul hath
condemned Polygamy as Adultery, and that the
early Chriſtians were not Polygamiſts, thoſe
Proofs will occur in the immediately ſubſequent
Obſervations.

Our Author, Page 380, again conſiders the
Paſſages of our Lord in the Goſpels of St.
Matthew and Mark, reſpecting Divorce and
Polygamy, and repeats the Aſſertion, that our
Lord was not laying down a new Law; and that
had he attempted any Thing oppoſite to the
Law of Moſes, he would have fallen into the
Snare of the Phariſees, who queſtioned him with
a View to reproach him as an Enemy to it.—
The Phariſees, proceeds our Author, attempted
no Reply, which would certainly not have been
the Caſe, had they underſtood him to have ſpo-
ken

ken againſt Polygamy; neither did his own Diſciples underſtand him to ſpeak of any Thing but Divorce; for their Concluſion is, "If the Caſe of a Man be ſo with his Wife, it is not good to marry;" *i. e.* if a Man cannot get rid of his Wife when he pleaſeth, he had better not marry at all. P. 384.—The Concluſion, ſaith our Author, muſt have been made from their underſtanding Chriſt to ſpeak of Divorce; for it is totally foreign from the Matter of Polygamy. How could they poſſibly mean that a Man had better have no Wife at all, if he could not have more than one at once? It muſt likewiſe be ſuppoſed that they did not miſunderſtand their Maſter; for if they had, he would doubtleſs have ſet them right in his Reply, and not have ſaid what clearly ſhews them to have underſtood him right."

In Reply to theſe Suggeſtions, be it obſerv'd, that the Phariſees attempted no reproachful Anſwer to our Lord's Prohibition of unjuſt Divorce, though they plainly underſtood that his Prohibition was contrary to rhe Moſaic Permiſſion. Why therefore ſhould our Author aſſert, that if they had underſtood our Lord to have

ſpoken

fpoken againft Polygamy, they would certainly have replied to him?

With refpect to our Lord's Difciples, the very Reply which our Lord made to their Conclufion, from which our Author afferts that it appears that they underftood him aright, evinceth that his Difcourfes related to both Polygamy and Divorce, or at leaft that the former was deducible from, and neceffarily implied in them.

Our Lord's Difciples fay, "If this be the Cafe between a Man and his Wife, it is not good to marry." But he faid to them, " All Men cannot receive this Saying, that it is not good to marry, but only they to whom it is given, or who are able to fubdue their Inclinations towards the conjugal State." If Polygamy was allowed as lawful by our Lord, and his Difciples had more than one Wife each, his Reply would not have been pertinent to their Interference. For in fuch Cafe, there would have been no Occafion to have faid, that ' all Men cannot receive this Saying,' fince, if one of a Difciple's Wives was difagreeable to him, he would have had others that would prevent his Inability to receive that Saying, or govern his

Incli-

Inclinations towards the conjugal Union. The Difciples, therefore, meant, not ' that they had better have no Wife at all, if they could not have more than one;' but that, as they could not have more than one Wife at once, they had better not marry, than be obliged to retain fuch a one as might render them un-happy.

The Conclufion, therefore, is by no means foreign to the Matter of Polygamy any more than to that of Divorce, but is evidently de-duced from their Obligation to have no more than one Wife at once, and undeniably evinceth, that they underftood our Lord's Dif-courfe to relate to both Polygamy and Di-vorce.

Our Author, in Page 385, affirms, that the Word *another*, in the Paffage, ' whoever fhall put away his Wife, except it be for Fornica-tion, and fhall marry another, committeth Adultery againft her,' muft agree with the an-tecedent γυναικα, or Wife; that therefore the Word *Wife* muft be underftood as following the Word αλλην, another, and this may be con-ftrued in the Senfe of αλλοτριαν γυναικα, *another*
Man's

Man's Wife; and this extraordinary Conftruction, he obferves, is confirmed by the firft
Epiftle to the Corinthians, in which the Word
αλλης is fo ufed, υπο αλλης συνειδησεως, being there
rightly tranflated, " another Man's Confcience." St. Paul, giving Directions concerning
the eating Things offered to Idols, recommends
the abftaining from them to avoid Offence, and
for Confcience-fake. ' Confcience, faith he, not
thine own, but of the others, who may be of-
fended; for, in Acts obvious to Obfervation,
this is to be recommended, but in what lies
between God and my Soul, why is my Liberty
judged of another Man's Confcience ?' υπο αλλης
συνειδησεως. Of what Service this Quotation can
be to our Author's Caufe, is to all who read it,
furely! a Problem. He cannot, certainly,
mean that the Word αλλης means *only* another
Man's Confcience, and that it doth not alfo
mean another *Woman's* Confcience! Or fhall we
fuppofe him to have adopted the Affertion that
Women have no Souls, and that therefore all
the Apoftles. Directions were only intended for
the Conduct of their Hufbands?

Our Author's Conftruction, and defigned
Limitation of the Senfe of this Paffage, can
neither

neither be defended by the original Words, nor general Tenor of the New Teſtament. For though the original Word, γυναικα, hath a Pronoun poſſeſſive coupled with it in the former Part of this Verſe, as γυναικα αυτȣ, and therefore is rightly rendered his Wife, yet, what Authority can we have from the latter Part of it, where we have only αλλην, to affirm, that, if we underſtand the Word γυναικα to follow it, it muſt alſo be coupled with a Pronoun poſſeſſive, or be underſtood as if it was? The Verſe, in Truth, will admit of no ſuch Conſtruction; nor could poſſibly, even with his utmoſt Violence, be preſſed into his Service. Whoſoever putteth away his Wife, except it be for Fornication, and marrieth another Wife, that is, *any* other Woman, be ſhe Virgin, or Widow, whom he ſhall make his Wife, committeth Adultery againſt her, is undeniably the moſt natural and obvious, and the only Senſe in which any impartial Reader of the Words can poſſibly underſtand them. Let us, by a familiar Inſtance, exhibit the Abſurdity of ſuch forced Interpretation as our Author hath adopted.

Suppoſe two Bankers or Merchants, Adventurers for Life, had articled, that no third

Perſon

Perfon fhould be admitted to a Partnerfhip in their Houfes, and according to fuch the original Defign of their Contract, it fhould by Deed be expreffed that, " Whofoever of them, without reafonable Caufe, fhall difmifs his Partner and article with another, committeth Injuftice againft him, &c. Would any Court of Juftice hefitate one Moment to pronounce the Party who fhould prefume to thus difmifs his Partner, and article with another, to be guilty of Injuftice, and liable to fuch Penalty as ought to be adjudged to fuch Procedure ?

Could the Offender, in this Cafe, exculpate himfelf by pleading, that he had not articled with one who had been unjuftly difmiffed from a Partnerfhip with others, but that he was one who had never before been in Bufinefs ?

Would any one who wanted not to make the Words of the faid Deed conform to his own Prejudices and Defigns, inftead of regulating his own Sentiments by it, ever dream of preffing fo plain, and exprefs a Declaration into his Service by offering fo great Violence to it? Would any impartial Reader ever conceive, that the Word, *another*, in ' Whofoever fhall
difmifs

difmifs his Partner, and article with another, muft mean, not any Man whatfoever, but only one who had before been *another Man's Partner?*

What an extraordinary Figure muft a Pleader make who fhould adopt our Author's Mode of Interpretation, and thus comment upon thefe Words! " Whofoever fhall, without reafonable Caufe, difmifs his Partner, and article with another, committeth Injuftice againft him." " The Word another, muft agree with the Antecedent, Partner; therefore the Word Partner muft be underftood as following the Word another, and this may be conftrued in the Senfe of another Man's Partner." " And therefore whofoever difmiffeth his Partner, and articles with another who hath not been in Bufinefs before, is not guilty of, or committeth no Injuftice againft him."

I am confident that Men in Bufinefs will view fuch Mode of Conftruction with no fmall Degree of Surprize, and not in the leaft be difpofed to thank our Author for fo *fhrewd* a Comment. Nor can it be conceived, as the facred Writings are our Rule of Sentiment and Conduct, that Society will acknowledge any Obligations for fuch Violence offered to them, fince,

G by

by fuch Meafures, they may be compelled to fubfcribe to the moft pernicious Pofitions that any partial Writer may chufe to advance. Indeed, fuch being our Author's Mode of Interpretation, it muft be confeffed, that after all his Harangues concerning popular Error, and his entertaining and anile Fables, not to forget that of the refpectable Whittington, we cannot give that Credit to his Judgment and Impartiality, to which his Imagination may fuggeft he hath a Right.

In Truth, after fuch our Author's Mode of Interpretation, we cannot even confider him, as he feems to reprefent himfelf, in his fecond Volume, in fo elevated and illuminated a Situation as ' the radiant Inhabitant of the Moon,' though as he hath been erecting Caftles in the Air, he may probably have had a more than ordinary Connexion with that Satellite. To this Suggeftion it is apprehended that fome, who confider his laudable Attempts to affert Polygamy, and recommend it to the Patronage of thofe in Power, may be inclined to fubfcribe, and at the fame Time applaud his Modefty, and *Diffidence,* when he afcribes to himfelf a peerlefs Infallibility, and reprefents all thofe who fhall prefume

to

to diffent from him, as fit to be only ranked with the Tribe of merely impotent Scoffers, Cavillers, and Objectors, perhaps unworthy of a Superiority to the prefumptuous Quadrupede that vainly " infulted the Glories of the peerlefs Reign of the Moon."—But to proceed.

Neither our Author's extraordinary Conftruction, nor the Practices of Divorce and Exchange of Wives that prevailed amongft the Jews and Pagans, can evince that a married Man could not be guilty of Adultery, unlefs his fecond Wife was a divorced Woman. This Truth we have already fufficiently evinced, but with a View to fome Suggeftions of our Author that have not been noticed, fhall repeat a Part of what hath been offered, with fome acceffional Obfervations refpecting them.

Our blefied Lord, in the Gofpels of St. Mark and St. Luke, declareth, that ' whofo marrieth her that is put away, committeth Adultery.' But thefe Words can by no Means evince, that the married Man who during the Life of his firft Wife marrieth another who was a Virgin or Widow, or any other fingle Woman, commith not Adul-

tery,

tery, there being no fuch particular Limitations in thefe or any other Paffages of our Lord and his Apoftles refpecting this Subject. The Suggeftions of our Author and others upon this Point, are merely conjectural, unfupported by any particular Evidence, and contrary to the various Declarations of the New Teftament.

Our bleffed Lord exprefsly declareth in St. Matthew's Gofpel, that whofoever fhall put away his Wife, except it be for Fornication, and fhall marry another, committeth Adultery :—and in St. Mark's Gofpel, that whofoever fhall put away his Wife and marry another, committeth Adultery againft her.—Here are evidently no Limitations of Adultery to the alone Inftance of a married Man marrying a divorced Woman, or another Man's Wife, but the Words are obvioufly general. The Word, *another*, evidently being a general Term, and denoting any other Woman, be fhe Virgin or Widow, any Woman whom he fhall prefume to take as a Wife during the Life of his firft. Our Author fuggefts, Page 374, that had our Lord intended to have

con-

condemned thofe who were guilty of Polygamy, " he would fcarcely have made Ufe of Words which do not defcribe their Situation,. but of Words that did. It is very plain, proceeds he, that he that putteth away his Wife by giving her a Bill of Divorcement, could have nothing to do with the Man who took two Wives toge- ther, or one to another, and cohabited with both." But, furely! it is very plain that who- foever putteth away his Wife and marrieth ano- ther, committeth Adultery, *hath* fomething to do with the Man who took two Wives together, as well as with him who fhould unlawfully di- vorce them. Had not our Author ended the Quotation at the Word *Divorcement*, and given us but a *Part* of the Verfe, the Reader muft have feen that it *had* fomething to do with the Polygamift; and this being the Cafe, our Lord hath ufed Words defcriptive of his Situation.

Before our Author had attempted the precife Limitation of thefe Words to the Cafe of Di- vorce alone, he fhould have been able to have evinced that Divorce and Exchange of Wives were the *only* Practices of the Jews and Pagans at the Time of our Lord's Incarnation, and thence have deduced that fuch Practices muft be the

only

only Objects of thefe Difcourfes, and that con-
fequently Divorce alone was the Subject intended by them. But our Author will acknowledge that the Hiftory of that Period evinceth,
that not only Divorce and Exchange of Wives,
but a Community of Women and Polygamy,
or Fornication and Adultery, were the Practices
of that Age : and, therefore, without ' interpret-
ing Scripture according to our own Conceits,
but by confidering the Times when, Places
where, and Situations of the Perfons to whom
it was addreffed,' we farther deduce, that they
afford no Ground for fuch Limitation as our
Author would fix upon them.

With refpect to the general Tenor of the
New Teftament, nothing can be more inconfiftent with it than our Author's extraordinary
Limitation. The New Teftament gives no
more Power to a married Man to marry another
Woman, during the Life of his firft Wife, than
it gives to a Wife to marry another Man during the Life of her firft Hufband. St. Paul
exprefsly commands both Hufband and Wife,
to continue inviolably, and intirely appropriate
to each other.

2

To

To avoid Fornication, faith he, as before
obferved, let every Man have his own Wife,
and let every Woman have her own proper
Hufband; let the Hufband render to the Wife
due Benevolence, and likewife alfo the Wife to
the Hufband: The Wife hath not Power over
her own Body, but the Hufband; and likewife
alfo, the Hufband hath not Power over his
own Body, but the Wife. Defraud ye not
therefore one another, &c. The Rights of
both Wife and Hufband are here declared to
be equal, the Hufband hath not Power over his
own Body, but the Wife; the Wife hath not
Power over her own body, but the Hufband.
If it be urged that the Hufband may yet, according to thefe Words, divide his Attention,
and have more Wives than one, it may be alfo
urged, that the Wife may divide *her* Attention,
and have more *Hufbands* than one. To ferioufly
affirm that each may fo do, is to be ferioufly
abfurd; and affert that both Hufband and
Wife have, and have not, the Power over each
others Perfons, at the fame Time. If tne
Wife hath Power over the Perfon of her Hufband he cannot confer it upon another Woman;
and if the Hufband hath Power over the Perfon

of

of his Wife, fhe cannot transfer it to another Man.

The Wife, under the Difpenfation of the Gofpel, may certainly plead the fame Rights, in that Refpect, as her Hufband, the Apoftle having made no fort of Difference in the Cafe before us. And our Saviour alfo fpeaks the fame Truth: for he not only declares, that if a Woman fhall put away her Hufband, and marry another, *fhe* committeth Adultery; but alfo that whofoever fhall put away his Wife, except for Fornication, and marry another, committeth Adultery againft her. Mark 10.

The Paffages of the New Teftament, re-fpecting the Laws of Matrimony, therefore, declare the Rights of both Hufband and Wife, to be equal, as to the Point before us, and ex-clude all Pretence for fuch Limitation as fome, by forced and erroneous Expofitions, would ex-tort from them.

I fhall difmifs this Point with the fubfequent farther Obfervations upon our Author's extra-ordinary Conftruction of the former Part of the ninth Verfe of the nineteenth of St. Matthew.

Our

Our Author defiring to affert the Privilege
of a married Man marrying any Woman except
another Man's Wife; let us juft remark the
Abfurdity of fuch Limitation, and affert the
Rights of the Wife, by tranflating a fimilar
Paffage of St. Mark, according to our Author's
Mode of Conftruction.

The Word, *another*, in whofoever fhall put
away his Wife and marry another, faith our
Author, ' muft agree with the Antecedent;
Wife; therefore the Word, *Wife*, muft be underftood as following the Word, *another*; and
may be rendered in the Senfe of another Man's
Wife.'

According to fuch Tranflation of this Paffage of St. Matthew, let us tranflate the following Paffage of St. Mark: ' If a Woman
fhall put away her Hufband, and marry another, fhe committeth Adultery.'

The Word *another*, fay we, muft here agree
with the Antecedent, ανδρα, or *Hufband*; therefore the Word *Hufband* muft be underftood as
following the Word αλλω, or *another*, and this
may be conftrued another Woman's Hufband.

H   Accord-

According to fuch Mode of Interpretation, therefore, our Lord's Words can here only mean that, if a Woman fhall put away her Hufband and marry another Woman's Hufband, fhe committeth Adultery: and the plain and obvious Inference deducible from this Interpretation is, that our Wives may put us away, and at once marry as many other Men as they pleafe, provided they are not the Hufbands of other Women, without being guilty of Adultery.

Such forced and unwarrantable Interpretations of Scripture may, perhaps, be permitted to evince the Abfurdity of them; but, furely! fhould, in all other Inftances, be cautioufly avoided, left the Ignorant be deceived, and the Vicious encouraged to perfevere in a Conduct that may prove fatal to their moft important Interefts.

With refpect to the Confideration of the Law of Mofes, the divine Permiffions extended to thofe who were under it, and other Suggeftions of this Writer before us, they exceed the Limits of my Defign; which was, to confider only the Paffages of the New Teftament,

ment, refpecting the Laws of Marriage, that
he hath erroneoufly interpreted; and evince
that Polygamy, allowed under the old Teftament, is prohibited by Chrift and his Apoftles;
becaufe upon their Authority alone, depends
the Truth of that Point here treated.

Our Author, however, having endeavoured
to deduce the Lawfulnefs of Polygamy from
the Mofaic Permiffion of it, and our Lord's
Declarations that he came not to deftroy the
Mofaic moral Law, but to fulfil it, I fhall conclude what hath been offered, with fome Obfervations refpecting fuch this Writer's Deduction.

The Laws of the Old and New Teftament
certainly afford a complete Rule of Sentiment
and Conduct. But yet, as, according to our
Author's Affertion, the Law of Mofes permitted Polygamy and unjuft Divorces, and Polygamy and unjuft Divorces are prohibited by
the Gofpel, we cannot but in thofe Refpects,
amongft others, confider the Gofpel as a more
perfect, explicit, and complete Rule of Sentiment, and Conduct, than the Law; and, con-
H 2   fequently,

fequently, than any that was ever before vouchfafed to Mankind.

Our bleffed Lord, exhorting to Beneficence,
and reproving the Pharifees for their Derifion,
and undue Attachment to fecular Purfuits, ac-
quaints them, that a Difpenfation was opening
to the World, that would prove adequate to
the Conviction of their Errors, and a perfect
and effectual Rule of Behaviour.

' The Law and the Prophets, faid he, were
until John; fince that Time, the Kingdom of
God is preached, and every one preffeth into
it.'

Yet, it is eafier for Heaven and Earth to pafs
away, than for one Tittle of the Law to fail.

And then, to evince that he meant to advance and perfect, and not deftroy or impair
the Law, he added that ' Whofoever puts
away his Wife, and marries another, commits
Adultery.' Luke 16.

Our Lord's Defign in thefe Paffages, evidently, is to fuggeft that he and John had re-
veale̹d

vealed a more excellent Rule of Sentiment and
Conduct than that afforded by the Law and Prophets: that he and John had prefcribed more
noble Precepts refpecting Benevolence and Beneficence, and a proper Contempt of the World,
than could be found in the Law or Prophets;
who endeavoured to influence Men to the Per-
formance of their Duty in general, by only tem-
poral Motives. The Kingdom of God is now
preached, faid he, and every one preffeth into
it; being fuperior to the Influence of fecular
Objects, and animated by the moft undoubted
Affurances of endlefs Blifs and Glory. And,
as a farther Inftance in Proof of this Truth, as
well as that he came to perfect the Law of
Mofes, he faid, that ' Whofoever puts away
his Wife and marrieth another, commits Adultery; and whofoever marrieth her that is put
away from her Hufband, commits Adultery:'
intimating that the Law permitted unjuft Divorces, but the Gofpel expreffly forbids them.
And, in the Verfe immediately preceding,
obviating any Suggeftion refpecting his having
a Defign to deftroy the Law, he declared, that
' Heaven and Earth fhould fooner pafs away,
than one Tittle of the Law fail;' according to
his Declarations in other Paffages, that he came

not

ot to deſtroy the Law, but to fulfil it; that in-
ſtead of abating the Force of it, he, as in the
Inſtances adduced, came πληρωσαι, to fulſil, advance, perfect, and complete it.

Our bleſſed Lord was the true Light that enlighteneth every Man that cometh into the
World, or, according to the Hebrew Mode of
ſpeaking, every Man that is born of Woman.
He was the true Light that enlighteneth every
Man, both Jews and Pagans, πανΊα ανθρωπον ερχομενον εις το κοτμον, and came idto the World, not
ſurely to perform what was unneceſſary, and
only what Moſes had *already* done? If this had
been the Caſe, if Moſes had ſufficiently en-
lightened every Man, how could the Evangeliſt
here ſtile our Savour, το Φως αληθινον ο Φωτιζει παντα
ανθρωπον ερχομενον εις το κο;μον, the true Light that
enlighteneth all Men, both Jews and Gentiles,
that come into the World?

Our Lord is certainly the true and only Light
that *duly* enlighteneth every Man that cometh
into the World. For he alone hath brought
Life and Immortality to *full* Light, afforded
us the moſt undoubted Aſſurances of eternal
Happineſs in a future State, and ſhewed us the

2   Way

Way that will infallibly lead to it, by prefcribing fuch a perfect and complete Rule of Sentiment and Conduct, as was never before his Incarnation revealed to Mankind.

Our Saviour came not to deftroy the typical, prophetic, or moral Part of the Law, but to fulfil what was typified by the Law, and foretold by the Prophets, to affert the full and fpiritual Import of the Mofaic moral Law, and to advance and complete it. Our Author having afferted, that Polygamy was permitted by the Mofaic Law, and therefore not immoral, can have no Pretence upon fuch Suppofition to affirm, that our Lord, by prohibiting Polygamy, hath deftroyed one Tittle of the moral Law of Mofes. For if Polygamy, permitted by Mofes, be not immoral, and therefore hath no relation to the moral Law, our Lord by prohibiting Polygamy, cannot have deftroyed any Part of that Law.

Our Author fuggefts in Page 323, that if we affert that our Saviour hath revived an old, or exhibited a new Law, refpecting Marriage, we fhall adopt the Errors of Socinius and Mahomet, who affirmed that the Law of Mofes was abrogated

abrogated by Chrift and others, and that a new
and more excellent Law than that of Mofes is
now prefcribed to our Conduct.

As our Writer is particularly fond of deducing
Confequences as Difcouragements to the Adop-
tion of Truths that militate againft him, it may
be neceffary, previoufly to the Reply to the Suggeftions before us, to declare that the Author of
thefe Obfervations upon the Treatife on Female
Ruin, is as fincere a Friend to the Proteftant
Religion, and as remote from Heterodoxy, as
the Writer of that Treatife can poffibly be:
that the Author of thefe Obfervations hath as
great a Regard for the Fair Sex, and ever was
as much inclined to the conjugal Union as any
the fincereft Votary of Hymen exifting : that
the Author of thefe Obfervations is at this Time,
and many Years hath been, a married Man:
and that though his Situation is fuch as might
render him fuperior to ordinary Reftraint, yet
hath he ever adhered to, and obferved the eftab-
lifhed Laws of Marriage, from Motives of Regard to the Injunctions of revealed Religion refpecting it.

With

With refpect to our Author's Suggeftions, that
if we affert that Chrift hath exhibited a new
Law relating to Marriage, we muft adopt the
Errors of Socinus or Mahomet, who affirmed
that the Law of Mofes was abrogated, and that
our Lord and others had introduced a new Law
more excellent than the former ; furely we may
remark, that our Writer hath exonerated *himfelf*
from all Imputation of that Infanity which he
feems willing to indirectly afcribe not only to
Infidels, but alfo to all fincere Chriftians who
diffent from him. For, whereas he juftly obferves with Mr. Locke, that ‘ Madnefs is ufually
allowed to be fo far confiftent with itfelf, as to
argue right from wrong Principles,’ and hath
moft certainly properly applied this Obfervation
to the impious Attempts of Socinus: yet hath
our Author, in the Suggeftions before us, not
argued *right* from *wrong* Principles, but, confiftently with *himfelf*, argued wrong, from right
Principles. We contend not that the moral
Law is abrogated, but that our Lord hath per-
fected it, and exhibited a new Command, prohibiting Polygamy ; and how fuch an Affertion
can entitle thofe who adopt it to the Denomi-
nations of Socinians, Mahomedans, or Mad-

I   men,

men, muſt ſurely be a Problem that cannot eaſily be ſolved.

We are certainly obliged to obſerve the moral Precepts of the Moſaic Law, in all Inſtances where it correſponds with thoſe of the Goſpel, but muſt ingenuouſly confeſs that if, in any Inſtance, it differeth from that of the Goſpel, or permits what the Goſpel prohibits, we, as Chriſtians, muſt give the Preference to the latter. The Moſaic Law, according to our Author, permits Polygamy; we are convinced that the Chriſtian Law prohibits it: we are therefore indiſpenſably obliged to obey the latter, though its Injunctions are contrary to ſuch Moſaic Permiſſion. As to our Author's Suggeſtions reſpecting the Immutability of the Law of Moſes, and our Lord's Intention never to aſſume Authority to abrogate it, but only to fulfil all Righteouſneſs, atteſt the Perfection of the Law, and illuſtrate and explain it—Our bleſſed Lord certainly came to diveſt the Law of the falſe Interpretations of the Jews, and to explain, perfect, and complete it; and therefore if there be any Improvement, or Alteration of that Law, or any Revival of an old Law, or any new Precept exhibited in the Goſpel, all Chriſtians, knowing

knowing them, are indifpenfably obliged to obferve them.

The Plea of the Immutability, or Perpetuity of the Law of Mofes, cannot excufe us if we are guilty of Polygamy under the Difpenfation of the Gofpel; the Mofaic Permiffion of Polygamy could not be intended to be perpetual, becaufe Chrift and his Apoftles have abro-gated it, and no Chriftian can pretend to indulge a Liberty that they have prohibited. The Lawfulnefs of unjuft Divorce might as well be deduced from the Immutability and Perpetuity of the Law of Mofes, as that of Polygamy. Our bleffed Lord declared, that not one Tittle of the Law fhould fail, and that he came not to deftroy, but fulfil it; yet he hath moft exprefsly abrogated the Permiffion of Divorce in thofe Inftances in which it was permitted by Mofes.

Our Saviour certainly ' founded his Claim to the Character of the Meffiah on the Old Teftament, and never affumed Au.hority to abrogate the moral Law of Mofes;' but yet he hath per-fected and completed it, and enacted a Law contrary to the Permiffion of Divorce and Po-

I 2 lygamy,

lygamy, without impeaching his own Veracity, or deſtroying the Moſaic Syſtem of Morals. Our Lord, certainly, might proteſt againſt all Intention to aboliſh the Moſaic Inſtitutes, and yet, without any Impeachment of his Veracity, illuſtrate, perfect, and complete them; for, ſurely, Completion and Abolition are not ſynonymous Terms!

Our Saviour ſubmitted to the Baptiſm of John, to filfil all Righteouſneſs, to own the Inſtitutions, comply with the Precepts, and juſtify the Wiſdom of God in ſending John to prepare his Way, by calling Men to Repentance.

In the 11th of Saint Matthew, our Saviour ſaith of St. John, that he was more than a Prophet; that none had riſen greater than John; and yet, that he who is leaſt in the Kingdom of Heaven, that the leaſt Prophet under the Diſpenſation of the Goſpel, is greater than he.— John is here repreſented as ſuperior to all ancient Prophets, on account of his Knowledge of the Myſteries of the Goſpel, his Teſtimony to Chriſt, and the Succeſs of his Labours, as well as his having been foretold by ancient Prophecy, and his miraculous Birth; yet, ſaith our Lord, he who is leaſt in the Kingdom of Heaven, is greater than he; the meanest Preachers of the Christian Religion shall, in general, receive greater Supplies of the Spirit, and the Knowledge of many important Truths of the Gospel, of which John was ignorant.

Our blessed Lord certainly came into the World to fulfil all Righteousness, to prescribe a complete Rule of Faith and Conduct, yet to do nothing of himself, but to preach the Doctrines of his Father, and teach as he gave him. Commandment. John 12.—But can it be inferred from these Truths, that, as our Author suggests, our Lord could not intend, or have Power to prohibit Polygamy? No. The obvious Inferences from hence are, not that Christ by prohibiting Polygamy hath abrogated one Tittle of the Law, but only that he hath fulfilled, perfected and completed it; and that, as he taught as his Father gave him Commandment, his Prohibition of Polygamy, and all his Injunctions and Prohibitions, are agreeable to the divine Will.

The Law of Moses, notwithstanding our Author's Suggestions, most certainly never commanded Polygamy; the Mosaic Law respecting

4   Seduction,

Seduction, by no Means expreſſly commanding
Polygamy, nor indiſputably extending to every
Man; and our Saviour could not abrogate
what never ſubſiſted. Our Lord hath revived
an old or advanced a new Law reſpecting Marriage, and aboliſhed the Permiſſion of
Polygamy, but, by no means, hath deſtroyed
any Law of Moſes that commanded it; becauſe
no ſuch Law ever ſubſiſted.

Our Saviour certainly atteſted the Excellence
of the Law when he declared, that there is no
Commandment greater than thoſe reſpecting
our Love to God and Man.

The Commandment reſpecting our Love of
God, is the principal and fundamental Command of the Law, and that to which all other
are reducible and ſubordinate. The Law reſpecting the Love of our Neighbour is alſo like
unto it. Every Duty to Man is reducible to,
and will neceſſarily reſult from this Principle.
The Law and the Prophets depend upon theſe
Commandments, it being the Intention of all
Revelation to promote them.

Grant

Grant we, therefore, thefe Truths alfo that our Lord, as before obferved, hath divefted the Law of the falfe Interpretations of the Jews, fully explained it, and declared that he came to fulfil it; let us even alfo indulge our Author with his Affertion that, when our Lord faid he had given to his Difciples a *new* Command-ment, that Commandment which is particu-larly ftiled the Law of *Chrift*, he meant only to eftablifh, and more powerfully enfore, an *old* Commandment; yet what Advantage can pof-fibly be derived from thefe Conceffions, to our Author's Caufe? Will thefe Conceffions evince, that becaufe our Lord came not to abolifh the Mofaic moral Law, he could not fulfil, perfect, and complete it? Will they evince, that he could not forbid a Practice that Mofes had ne-ver enjoined? Becaufe they are inconfiftent with an Intention to abrogate the Law, can they alfo be inconfiftent with a Defign to prohibit Poly-gamy, which the Law never commanded?

If our Author would effectually advance his Purpofe, it fhould be recollected that it will be incumbent upon him to not only exhibit unquef-tionable Evidence againft the Abrogation of the Mofaic Permiffion of Polygamy, but alfo to produce

produce an *exprefs* Command of Polygamy from
the Law of Mofes. Previoufly to the Impeachment of our Lord's Veracity, who protefted againft
the Abolition of the Law, diligent Search after the
Command of Polygamy fhould be made amongft
the Mofaic Inftitutes; and if our Author's Imagination fhould fuggeft to him, that the *de-
firable* Injunction hath not eluded his In-
quiry, he will have the Satisfaction of conceive-
ing that he is intitled to no trifling Acknowledg-
ments from many *well-difpofed* People, whofe
Minds have hitherto been filled with Matters of
fore Reftraint, by thofe of our Commentators
who were incapable of fuch *deep*, and *beneficial*
Inveftigation. Nor hath our Author Reafon to
apprehend, that the Refult of fuch *laudable* In-
quiries can prove, in the leaft, inconfiftent with
his Profeffions as a Freethinker in thefe Points,
or as a *Friend* to the Law, and an Enemy to
vulgar Prejudice, and Preconception. For the
utmoft Confequences of the Inveftigation of a
Mofaic Injunction of Polygamy, can prove
only that Mofes commanded all Votaries
of **H**ymen not merely to look with Defire
after, but to freely have perfonal Intercourfe
with, and, at once, marry as many
Women

Women as they pleafed; and that all irregular Defire and Commerce between the Sexes,
and Adultery and Seduction, inftead of being
cenfurable, were commendable and virtuous,
under the Mofaic Difpenfation. But, *amato
ludo,* it muft be ingenuoufly confeffed, that
fuch our Author's Refearches would be intirely
unneceffary; for could the Refult of them prove
an exprefs Command of Polygamy, yet, as before obferved, we as Chriftians, muft ftill be
indifpenfibly obliged to adhere to the Injunctions of the Gofpel which expreffly forbid it.

But to proceed. Chrift hath, certainly, reduced the Law of Marriage to its primitive Inftitution, and abrogated all Permiffion of Polygamy, and unjuft Divorce. Chrift, therefore,
hath prohibited, what our Author afferts was
before permitted or difpenfed with; and yet
acted confiftently with his Declaration, that he
came not to deftroy, but to fulfil, advance and
complete the Law: The Law of Mofes was
primarily addreffed to, and intended for, the
Jews; and our Saviour hath perfected, advanced and rendered it, by the *Acceffion* of the
Gofpel, a moft complete Rule of Faith and Conduct to all Mankind.

K

To

To thefe Truths it is prefumed our Author will readily fubfcribe, unlefs he would avow a Purpofe to advance the Doctrines and Commands of the Old Teftament to a Superiority over thofe of the New, or at leaft to an Equality with the Gofpel as an univerfal Rule of Sentiment and Conduct, to which the Old Teftament afferts no Claim.

Our Author afferts, that the Prohibition of Polygamy by our Lord, would prove an Impeachment of the divine Wifdom and Prefcience, ' as arguing an Imbecility or Weaknefs ' of Underftanding and Knowledge, like that ' of human Legiflators, who make Laws to ' remedy Evils as they arife before them, but ' cannot tell what a Day may bring forth; and ' therefore repeal at one Time, the Law which ' they made at another.' Page 363.—This, it is confeffed, is a pretty ftrong Affertion, and feems to border upon fomething worfe than Infanity.

However, the Abfurdity of this Suggeftion is adequate to its Strength and Confidence. For nothing can be more evident, than that fuch a Prohibition of Polygamy is fo remote from all

Impeach-

Impeachment of the divine Wifdom and Prefcience, as to be entirely confonant with that
Wifdom which hath ever been vifible and ad-
mired in God's Regulation and Government of
Mankind, and particularly in his revealing Doctrines and enacting Laws according to the Capacities and Situations of his Creatures, as they
could bear them.

It becomes not finite Beings upon Earth to
pretend to affign with Certainty the Reafons of
divine Permiffions; various Solutions have been
attempted, that fome have adopted, others re-
jected, as muft be the Cafe where Revelation
hath not afforded any exprefs Declaration, or
fufficient Light refpecting them. But, though
we have no exprefs Declaration of Scripture
concerning the Affertions before us, yet have
we certain Facts evincing the Abfurdity and
Error of them.

Our Author in the Paffages tranfcribed, and
in thofe immediately preceding, hath confidently
affirmed, that " It is as *impoffible* that Chrift
" fhould condemn Polygamy as Adultery, as
" that he fhould allow Adultery as lawful Com-
" merce; and that to fuppofe God to ever re-

" voke,

" voke, alter, or change the moral Inftitutes of
" the Old Teftament, is to fuppofe fome Defect
" in the Deity, and impeach his Wifdom and
" Prefcience." Page 363.

Would not any Reader unacquainted with the
Scriptures, infer from fuch confident, not to fay
impious Affertions of a Preacher of the Gofpel,
that no Inftance of the Alteration or Repeal of
any divine Inftitutions and Laws can poffibly
be produced from the facred Writings?

Our Author's afferting the Immutability of
the Law, and denying even Chrift or the Deity
a Power to revoke, alter, or perfect his moral
Inftitutes, induce one to think, that this Writer
hath adopted certain metaphyfical Pofitions,
which, by ufurping the Place of Truth, often
prove the Source of pernicious Error. We muft
fuppofe our Author to have fo long dwelt upon
the eternal and unalterable Fitnefs and Unfitnefs
of Things, as to have conceived all Change of
them an Impoffibility: when after all abftract
Reafonings and Harangues upon thefe Points,
nothing is more evident than that Things are
only fit, or unfit, as they relate to the Capacities, Situations, and Condition of Mankind;
and

and thefe Circumftances changed or altered, that which was before fit, becomes unfit, and that which before was innocent and virtuous, is now criminal and vicious.

I fhall conclude what hath been offered, with one Inftance, amongft others that might be adduced, that evince the Deity to have altered and even revoked, as well as permitted the Violation of his Inftitutions and Laws, according to the Capacities, Condition, and Situations of Mankind.—God exprefsly commanded our firft Parents, and their immediate Succeffors, to increafe and multiply, at a Time when their Situation was fuch that they could not obey this Law, without committing an Act which by a fubfequent Law hath been prohibited as a Sin of the deepeft Dye.

All perfonal Intercourfe between Brother and Sifter, is exprefsly forbidden by the Levitical Law; and nothing is more feverely reprobated and condemned, in the New Teftament, than the inceftuous Commerce of the Sexes.

God's Command refpecting Population by Perfons nearly related, hath therefore been abro-

gated

gated by both the Old and New Teftament, the Deity having, fince their Promulgation, prohibited what before he permitted and enjoined. Nor can fuch Prohibition, in the leaft, impeach the Wifdom or Knowledge of the Deity, fince the Circumftances and Situation of Mankind, at firft, rendered fuch Permiffion indifpenfably neceffary.——We therefore can fafely affirm, that it is *not* impoffible that the Deity fhould alter or revoke, or repeal at one Time the Law that he made at another.

T H E E N D,

www.ingramcontent.com/pod-product-compliance
Lightning Source LLC
Chambersburg PA
CBHW020232090426
42735CB00010B/1653